Acknowledgements

This research was supported by a grant from the Gatsby Charitable Foundation. We would like to thank Diane Bushnell and Colin Chalmers for invaluable statistical advice and support, Ann Richardson for helpful editorial guidance and Geoff Shepherd and Vida Field for sharing their knowledge and experience with us. We are also grateful to Patricia Louis and Karen Lorimer for the dedicated administrative support provided to the project.

Making Community Mental Health Teams Work

CMHTs and the People who Work in Them

By Steve Onyett, Tracey Pillinger and Matt Muijen

© The Sainsbury Centre for Mental Health 1995

ISBN: 1 870480 17 1

Published by
The Sainsbury Centre for Mental Health
134 – 138 Borough High Street
London
SE1 1LB

0171 403 8790

Table of Contents

1 Introduction

Community Mental Health Teams (CMHTs) are a central component of most local services for people with mental health problems. Composed of professionals from a wide range of disciplines, they are intended to provide an effective local mental health service that prioritises those whose problems are severe and long-term. But what do they actually do, and how do they work as a team? What helps or hinders a team in focusing on people with severe and long-term mental health problems? How is team membership experienced by different staff? This report sets out the results of research addressed to these questions.

This study entailed two distinct elements. First, a national survey explored the organisation and operation of CMHTs in England. A separate publication has described its results in some detail and therefore, we only highlight some key findings here[1]. Second, we carried out a postal survey of team members in 60 of these CMHTs to examine job satisfaction and burnout among staff. This survey also examined caseloads and how often service users were seen, how clear team members were about the role of the team and their own role within it, and their identification with the team and their profession. We also explored their principal sources of rewards and job pressure, as a particular aim of this research was to examine the features associated with job satisfaction or burnout among staff. Further details of the research methods are provided in Appendix 2.

The study was intended to complement earlier research on CMHTs. Much has been written about different models of CMHTs[2] and there are a number of studies of individual projects set up with special Government funds to target specific client groups.[3] But aside from one survey of CMHTs based in community mental health centres carried out by The Sainsbury Centre for Mental Health in 1987–8[4], little is known of how CMHTs with ordinary histories and no special funding are organised.

2 Community Mental Health Teams

Community mental health teams can be defined in a number of ways. For this study, we defined a CMHT as a team of four or more members, from two or more disciplines, that is recognised as a CMHT by service managers, serves adults with mental health problems as its identified client group, does most of its work outside hospitals (although it may be hospital-based) and offers a wider range of services than simply structured day care. We excluded teams that are wholly dedicated to people over 75, those with drink or drug problems or people with learning difficulties from the study.

In total, we identified 517 CMHTs in 144 District Health Authorities (DHAs), representing nearly all (96%) DHAs in England. A questionnaire was sent to each of these, of whom 302 replied (a 58% response rate). The following information is based on the 302 CMHTs taking part in the survey.

The average size of the CMHTs surveyed was found to be 15 people, but as many people work only part-time, this equals an average of 11 full-time equivalents (FTEs). Details of teams' composition are given below.

The Location of CMHTs

Figure 1 sets out the location of the CMHTs surveyed. It can be seen that the most common location (45% of all teams) is a community mental health *centre* (CMHC). This is generally a building that provides a base for a multidisciplinary team, with a number of therapeutic activities on site. Since 1987–8, CMHCs have increased approximately three-fold in number. This might be a cause for concern, as they have often been criticised for vague and over-ambitious aims and a tendency to neglect those people with the most severe mental health problems[4,5].

Interestingly, given the community emphasis of CMHTs, the next most common location (14%) is a hospital site, although it was often stressed that this did not influence the work of the team.

Perhaps the most surprising finding is the very wide range of locations where CMHTs can be found. Nearly one third (31%) of the total are scattered across day centres or hospitals, resource centres, primary care, residential (in ordinary houses or institutional residential care settings) and 'other' (a mixture of office accommodation, sometimes shared with other agencies). It is also notable that 10% of teams are not based together at all.

Figure 1 – Team base location

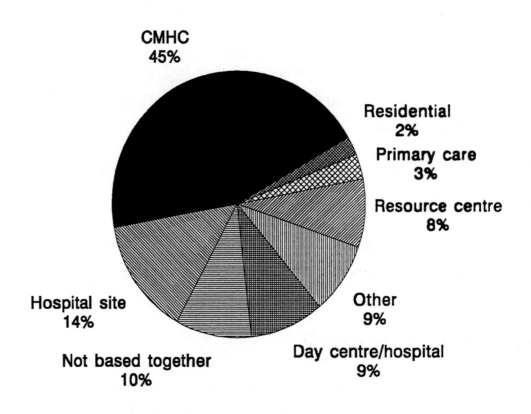

The Services Provided

Table 1 sets out the many services provided by CMHTs, starting with those most commonly offered. It can be seen that virtually all (90% or more) offer individual therapy or counselling, multidisciplinary direct work with users, individual service planning, consultation to mental health workers from other agencies and support or education for carers.

There is also evidence of clear attention to the needs of people with severe and long-term health problems.[6] The great majority (89%) indicate that they provide services particularly for this population. The survey of CMHCs[4] carried out by The Sainsbury Centre for Mental Health in 1987–8 found that very few offered services of obvious value to this group. At that time, only 12% offered support for carers, 11% provided occupational therapy and as few as 5% offered practical assistance with everyday problems. In contrast, many CMHTs are now offering these services; for example, most (89%) assess people's ability to do everyday activities (such as self care and using money) and more than two thirds (70%) offer practical 'hands-on' help with day-to-day problems (such as shopping or transport). Nearly half (46%) of the teams offer day care. This was highlighted by earlier research as an important component when aiming to serve people with severe and long-term mental health problems.[7]

Many CMHTs also aim their services to other specific groups. Two thirds (67%) suggested that they provide services for people who have not previously used mental health services and two fifths (42%) provide services particularly for women. Ethnic minority groups, in contrast, do not appear to be well-provided for, with only 13% of CMHTs providing services particularly for them.

The range of therapies provided is quite striking. In addition to those noted above, three quarters (75%) of CMHTs provide drug treatments, nearly as many (73%) provide group therapy and over two thirds (68%) provide family therapy or counselling. In addition, over half (56%) provide depot clinics. The great majority (85%) also claim to promote self-help.

However, some areas still show room for improvement. For instance, only one quarter (23%) of CMHTs are open after working hours and at weekends, although access at these times is often a priority for service users.[8] The teams providing such access usually have greater input from community support workers and non-CPN nurses and are most often based in community resource centres. They are least often found in primary care settings or CMHCs.

Community mental health teams are clearly associated with care in the community. But what happens when service users move into hospital? We found that all teams use in-patient beds and three quarters (73%) have direct access to beds via a team member. The latter tend to have a higher full-time equivalent complement of doctors.

Table 1 – Services provided by CMHTs

Service	% of CMHTs undertaking
Therapy or counselling for individuals	97
Multidisciplinary direct work with clients following assessment	94
Individual service planning	94
Consultation to mental health workers from other agencies	93
Support/education for carers	91
Services particularly for people with severe and long-term mental health problems	89
Assessment of activities of daily living (e.g. using money, personal hygiene, etc)	89
Promotion of self help	85
Multidisciplinary assessment: two or more disciplines at the same time	81
Formal assessments under the 1983 Mental Health Act	79
Training in activities of daily living	78
Drug treatments (other than depot clinics)	75
Publicising the service (i.e. more than just word of mouth)	74
Group therapy	73
Immediate response to crisis in the situation in which the crisis is happening	71
Practical 'hands-on' help with day-to-day problems (e.g. shopping, transport)	70
Therapy or counselling for families	68
Services particularly for people who have never used mental health services before	67
Physical space for outside agencies to use	58
Depot clinics	56
Public education (e.g. on preventing mental health problems)	48
Accommodation	48
Day care or other occupation	46
Drop in/walk-in/open-access facility	46
Services particularly for women	42
Services particularly for people whose behaviour services find 'challenging' or 'difficult to manage'	31
Work opportunities	24
Client access to team members after working hours and at weekends	23
Direct purchase of services by practitioners or case (or care) managers controlling budgets	17
Services particularly for people from specific ethnic groups	13

It is useful to make the distinction between *planning* and *providing* care for those in hospital. We found that the most common arrangement (42% of teams) is for responsibility for planning care to be transferred to in-patient staff, while the CMHT continues to provide care. Around one quarter (27%) of teams transfer responsibility for planning *and* providing care to hospital staff. Only 30% of teams retain responsibility for planning care for in-patients. This may contribute to the discontinuity of care between hospital and community services that was sadly so evident from the Clunis report.[9] Where responsibility for planning care is retained, there is a significantly higher full-time equivalent complement of social workers in the team.

How are the services of CMHTs accessed? Generally, CMHTs promote open access, with most (53%) accepting referrals from anyone. Self-referral is accepted by two thirds (68%) and the proportion is even higher (74%) among those based in CMHCs. In all, somewhat over half (57%) serve as the first contact point for all mental health referrals in their locality or sector.

Working as a Team

In some ways, CMHTs seem to operate as an integrated team. Nearly all (92%) meet as a team at least once a week. Well over half (57%) pool all referrals. Not surprisingly, this practice is most common where a large proportion of the team is based together and there is a single referral route into the team (e.g. via the team administrator or doctor).

In other respects, however, CMHTs do not always work in a fully integrated way. Roughly half (53%) of the teams take referrals via individual team members, rather than by a single referral route. Less than two fifths (38%) have a totally shared record-keeping system for information collected in work with service users. The same proportion (38%) share some of their records, such as individual service plans or assessments. In one quarter (26%) of teams, professions keep all their own records separately.

Care (or Case) Management

About half (52%) of all teams operate care (or case) management, as defined by the team. A much higher proportion (83%) operate keyworker systems, of whom roughly half (48%) also operate care management. Among the teams operating care or case management, most (86%) view it as one of a number of tasks to be undertaken by professional practitioners with other responsibilities. Only a small proportion (10%) report that those undertaking care management are solely care managers. This suggests that care management in mental health is being integrated into existing practice, rather than converting or recruiting staff to work solely as care managers. We suggest that this augurs well for the integration of health and social services practice. Indeed, it is encouraging that, since the survey, draft Government guidance has gone further than ever before in recommending that (social services-led) care management and the (health-led) Care Programme Approach be fully integrated[10].

The Management of CMHTs

There is a major shift among CMHTs towards having team managers or co-ordinators; three quarters have such an arrangement now, compared to only a small proportion (10%) of CMHCs in 1987–8. These team managers or co-ordinators usually have responsibility for the day-to-day management of the team, including liaising with senior management over team issues, organising evaluation or review, representing the team at public meetings and authorising leave. Their role is, therefore, clearly identified with operational management.

Despite this, we found that the 'team as a whole' is often seen as carrying most responsibility for key management tasks. For example, two fifths (43%) of the CMHTs report that the 'team as a whole' has most responsibility for deciding the client group of the team – a critically important strategic decision. This is the job of management or steering groups in only one quarter (23%) of teams and of individual managers or planners outside the team in a very small number (10%).

A related task is assessing the mental health needs of the local community. Again, the team as a whole is most often responsible (28% of teams), although individual managers or planners outside the team carry ultimate responsibility in a sizeable number of teams (22%).

The allocation of cases is undertaken by the team as a whole in roughly half (51%) the teams and in only one fifth (20%) by team co-ordinators or managers. The team as a whole also dominates when deciding which referrals the team accepts day-to-day (59%).

These findings suggest that despite the fact that so many CMHTs now have team managers or co-ordinators, ultimate responsibility for management tasks remains dispersed or undefined within the team, with little involvement from outside managers.

Clinical supervision highlights a key issue in multiprofessional teams: the relationship between operational and professional management. Clinical supervision would normally be regarded as the job of managers who share the same professional background. Yet this is true of only half the teams. In 15% of teams the team manager or co-ordinator is most often responsible for such supervision, and other individual team members in a further 15%.

There is a danger that where operational management is weak, the distinction between operational and professional management responsibilities will become blurred. This was stressed by one team member, lamenting the absence of a team manager/co-ordinator:

> 'No team management structure exists other than professional line management. Lack of a team manager/co-ordinator poses difficulties for the team and tends to reinforce the traditional role of consultant psychiatrist as team leader.'

In fact, the team's senior doctor rarely has ultimate responsibility for management tasks except in the area of 'over-ruling the decisions of team members if necessary' (21%). Even here, however, professional line managers are more often responsible (32%).

Are service users ever involved in management? As can be seen in Figure 2, we found that only a small number (8%) of CMHTs have routine user attendance in a decision-making role at either management/steering groups or business meetings. Nonetheless, one quarter (23%) suggested that they involve users in an advisory role and somewhat under half (43%) regularly survey users or collect information on their views. We note, however, that nearly three quarters of CMHTs have no plans to involve service users in management decision-making.

Although still very limited, such involvement has improved since the 1987–8 survey when only a very small proportion (12%) of CMHCs had any user involvement in management and only 16% indicated that they conducted user surveys.

Interestingly, teams are prepared to offer more responsibility to community members in general, both in an advisory capacity (25%) and in a decision-making role (17%). It must be noted that here, too, the proportions remain small.

Figure 2 – User and community member involvement in running CMHTs

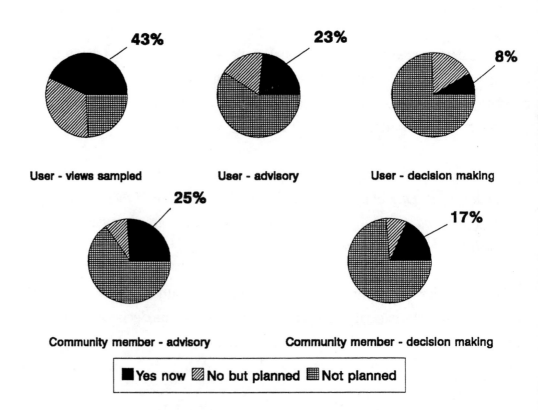

CMHTs and People With Severe and Long-Term Mental Health Problems

A key issue in this research was the extent to which CMHTs are focusing on people with severe and long-term mental health problems. We noted above that CMHTs are increasingly offering services of clear relevance to this population, with a high proportion (89%) suggesting that they provide services particularly for them. Indeed, it can also be noted that roughly one third (32%) indicated that they provide services particularly for people whose behaviour is deemed 'challenging' or 'difficult to manage'.

33% of CMHTs reported that two thirds or more of their caseload is dedicated to people with severe and long-term mental health problems. This may represent a shift towards work with this population among an increasing proportion of CMHTs, although the lack of an earlier survey does not allow us to make ready comparisons over time.

We were also interested in exploring the characteristics of teams which work with people with severe and long-term mental health problems. An analysis of the survey data suggests that they include the following features:

- **Urban (as opposed to suburban or rural) teams.**
  This might be predicted from the greater numbers of disadvantaged people in urban environments.[11]

- **Teams based in 'other' locations (mainly offices).**
  This suggests the value of a team base where service users are not seen for clinical work and where help is instead provided in ordinary environments, such as the person's home. This confirms the findings of earlier related research.[12]

  Primary care-based teams have the smallest proportion of clients with severe and long-term mental health problems. This may be partly due to large numbers of referrals from GPs of 'anxious and unhappy people with overwhelming social and domestic difficulties' rather than people with severe and long-term mental health problems.[13] To prevent teams becoming overwhelmed by inappropriate referrals, it might be better for them not to be based in primary care settings but for them to provide assessments and subsequent interventions there as necessary.

CMHC based teams, have the next lowest proportion of clients with severe and long-term mental health problems. This may be because of their traditional aim of providing a 'comprehensive' service whereby a wide variety of services are provided on-site to all comers.

- **Not offering the first contact point for all mental health referrals in the locality.**
  The fact that most CMHTs offer the first contact point for referrals may contribute to the neglect of people with severe and long-term mental health problems reported in earlier studies.[4,7]

Although being the first contact point is associated with caseloads containing a lower proportion of clients with severe and long-term mental health problems, accepting referrals from a wide range of sources is not. This suggests that it is not the range of people who can refer but *who they are referring and which people the team accepts* that is of central importance. In order to maintain a focus on people with the most severe mental health problems, services need to accept referrals from a wide range of sources but then 'gate-keep' to ensure that only the team's defined client group are taken on for assessment and on-going work.

- **Psycho-social interventions, such as out-of-hours access, work opportunities, practical help with everyday problems and assessment of skills in performing activities of daily living.**

- **Full-time dedication of posts to the team**.
  Teams with a larger proportion of people with severe and long-term mental health problems have significantly less part-time working among team members.[14] This may be because integrated teams provide reliable access to an appropriate range of skills, and the intensive and continuous community support

required for working with complex on-going difficulties. They also have clearer team boundaries, allowing the development of a strong team identity and peer support.

Team caseload composition is not related to the team's composition or its management. This is, perhaps, surprising, since it would be predicted that teams targeting people with severe and long-term mental health problems would be specifically composed of relevant disciplines, such as psychiatrists, nurses, occupational therapists and community support workers. This finding may indicate a lack of forethought on this matter by teams and an assumption of a standard team composition. Alternatively, it may reflect the influence of an unpredictable labour market on team recruitment.

Whether or not the team has a manager or co-ordinator bears no relationship to caseload composition. This may reflect the general abdication of management responsibily described above, resulting in a poor degree of focus on those with severe and long-term problems.

3 The Members of Community Mental Health Teams

Having examined what CMHTs do and how they function as a team, it is important to look at their constituent parts. We took particular interest in the experience of job satisfaction and the of burnout among team members.

Composition of Teams

First, it is necessary to examine the composition of CMHTs. As can be seen in Table 2, the most common disciplines are community psychiatric nurses (CPNs) (93%), social workers (86%) and administrative staff (85%). While consultant psychiatrists are also typically present, it is notable that one fifth (21%) of CMHTs do not have sessional input from a consultant psychiatrist.

Certain kinds of staff are not invariably members of teams. Both clinical psychologists (72%) and occupational therapists (69%) are relatively common, but community support workers are found in under two fifths (38%). While doctors other than consultants exist in over two thirds (68%), only one third of teams (34%) have nurses other than CPNs. Volunteers are relatively uncommon (in only 14% of teams).

Many staff are only part-time members of the team. The table also shows the mean full-time equivalent input of each discipline. It can be seen that, on average, teams had the equivalent of three and a half CPNs, but only two thirds of a consultant psychiatrist and half a clinical psychologist.

A similar picture emerges when the amount of part-time working is examined for each discpline.[15] Only CPNs and other nurses, social workers, occupational therapists and community support workers work on average more than four days per week (0.8 FTE) with the team.

This finding is not of solely academic interest. As noted above, the degree of part-time working in CMHTs is of considerable importance to whether the team serves people with severe and long-term mental health problems.

Part-time working, with its implication of lower team commitment, is also a concern among team members. The view that *'to be truly called a multidisciplinary team, one has to have equal commitment from all the services involved'* was typical. One person complained that all members had commitments elsewhere and there was concern about having to *'beg and borrow'* professional time. Social workers, psychologists and consultant psychiatrists were most often cited as lacking sufficient commitment to the team. Lack of team integration was also reflected in concern about diffuse team boundaries (e.g. with neighbouring rehabilitation teams).

Table 2 – Team composition

Discipline	% of teams containing discipline	Mean input per team FTEs (people)
Community psychiatric nurses	93	3.55 (3.83)
Social workers	86	1.53 (1.87)
Administrative staff (inc. receptionists)	85	1.32 (1.87)
Nurses (other than CPNs)	34	1.01 (1.22)
Occupational therapists	69	0.75 (0.95)
Community support workers*	38	0.65 (0.88)
Consultant psychiatrists	79	0.62 (1.02)
Doctors (other than consultants)	68	0.59 (1.34)
Clinical psychologists	72	0.50 (0.90)
Others	28	0.36 (0.57)
Other specialist therapists	32	0.21 (0.44)
Volunteer staff	14	0.07 (0.45)

* The term community support worker includes generic mental health workers, the term which was used on the questionnaire

We examined whether teams providing particular services have more input from specific disciplines. Predictable associations emerged, with a higher complement of doctors where drug treatments, depot clinics, crisis intervention and Mental Health Act assessments are provided. Similarly, where there are more occupational therapists, there tends to be more assessment and training in activities of daily living, practical 'hands-on' help, day care or other occupation and services for women. A higher complement of clinical psychologists is associated with group therapy, the promotion of open access and services for women. Conversely, there is significantly less input from psychologists where teams provide services specifically for people whose behaviour was seen as 'challenging'.

Staff Satisfaction and Burnout

The following findings are based on our second postal survey of the members of 60 teams. Details of the methods employed are contained in Appendix 2. See the below for definitions of the terms used.

The Meaning Behind the Measures

Job satisfaction is a scale that examines staff satisfaction with*:

Achievement, value and growth: how the job taps skills, how efforts are valued, whether an individual can personally develop or grow in a job and there are enough career opportunities and scope for a person to achieve his/her ambitions;

The job itself, in terms of the tasks to be performed, the amount of work needing to be done and job security;

The team's design and structure, including the way information flows around the team, the way changes and innovations are implemented in the team and the way in which conflicts are resolved;

Organisational processes, including the degree to which a person feels 'motivated' by the job, the style of supervision used, the amount of participation given in important decision-making and the amount of flexibility and freedom a person feels to exist in the job;

Personal relationships in the team, including the psychological 'feel' or climate that dominates the team and the extent to which a person identifies with the public image or goals of the team.

Burnout has three dimensions:

Emotional exhaustion describes a feeling of being emotionally over-extended and exhausted;

Reduced personal accomplishment is experienced as decreased feelings of competence and achievement;

Depersonalisation is the development of unfeeling and impersonal responses to service users as a result of work stress.

Personal role clarity exists when a person is clear about his/her responsibilities, who he/she is accountable to and how his/her work will be evaluated.

Team role clarity refers to the extent to which the team is seen as having clear aims and priorities, including clarity about who it is trying to help; it also covers whether it is easy to tell if the team is doing its job right (or not).

Team identification refers to the extent to which a person feels a positive sense of belonging to a team. 'Identification' literally refers to a person's sense of who he/she is, i.e. self concept. Social identity theory suggests that people derive a sense of social identity through group membership and comparisons with other groups.

Professional identification refers to the extent to which a person feels a positive sense of belonging to his/her profession, or, where there is no professional background, the group sharing the same job designation.

for psychometric reasons the 'job itself' and 'organisational processes' sub-scales were not examined separately.

Job satisfaction

Figure 3 sets out job satisfaction across the range of disciplines surveyed.[16] Overall, it is significantly higher than that reported in a recent large-scale study in one DHA[17], but large differences can be seen across disciplines. In particular, consultants and other doctors are most satisfied, with social workers, community support workers and other workers least satisfied. These differences are explored in more detail below in the discussion on individual disciplines.

Figure 3 – Job satisfaction by discipline

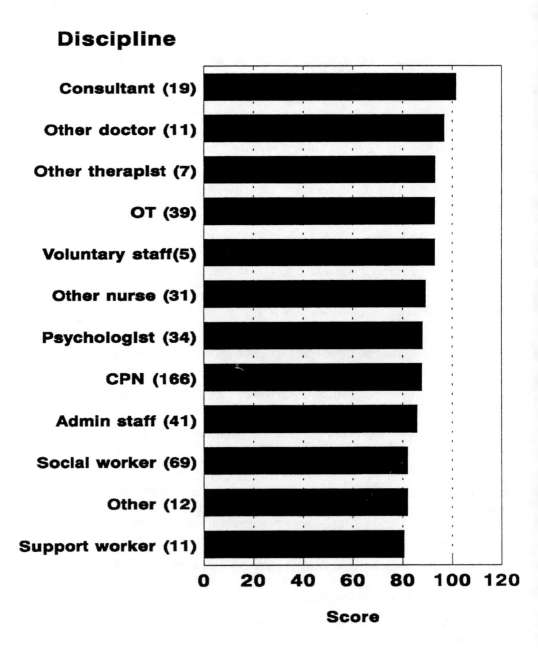

Burnout

Burnout is popularly considered as a syndrome of feeling emotionally over-extended and exhausted (emotional exhaustion), with decreased feelings of competence and achievement (personal accomplishment) and unfeeling and impersonal responses to service users (depersonalisation).[18]

Taking all the disciplines together, we found that, compared with the norms for mental health workers published by the scale authors[18], emotional exhaustion and a sense of personal accomplishment is significantly higher, while the experience of depersonalisation is significantly lower.[20] In other words, although staff overall do not appear to be experiencing detachment from service users or decreased feelings of competence and achievement, they are feeling significantly emotionally over-extended and exhausted. Emotionally exhausted staff also had lower job satisfaction.[19] This is consistent with another recent survey undertaken by The Sainsbury Centre for Mental Health.[8]

Table 3 shows the distribution of burnout in terms of 'high', 'moderate' or 'low' levels. This is based on the top, middle and bottom third of the distribution used for the scale norms. In other words, if our data were the same as the norms, then the percentages would all read 33%. Although overall there are more people than expected falling into the 'high emotional exhaustion' category (44%), there are fewer people with high burnout on the personal accomplishment (13%) and depersonalisation (18%) measures. There are, however, some important differences between disciplines which are described below.

Sick leave

Staff burnout and dissatisfaction might be reflected in high levels of sick leave. This is of obvious importance because of the dangers of discontinuity in support for service users, in addition to the cost of absences to the employing authority. In fact, we found an average 3 – 4 days reported sick leave in the previous six months. Just under half (47%) of those surveyed reported no absence, with slightly fewer (40%) taking one to five days. The number taking more than five days was relatively small (5% took six to ten days and 6% took more than ten days). Interestingly, there were no significant differences between disciplines. Rees & Cooper (1992) found that reported sick leave correlated highly with actual sickness absence (r=0.96)

Table 3 – Distribution of high, moderate and low burnout by discipline

Discipline	Emotional exhaustion			Personal accomplishment			Depersonalisation		
	High	Moderate	Low	High	Moderate	Low	High	Moderate	Low
Community psychiatric nurses	74 (44.6)	41 (24.7)	47 (28.3)	14 (8.4)	31 (18.7)	106 (63.9)	23 (13.9)	38 (22.9)	99 (59.6)
Nurses (other than CPNs)	16 (51.6)	7 (22.6)	8 (25.8)	2 (6.5)	2 (6.5)	25 (80.6)	7 (22.6)	9 (29.0)	14 (45.2)
Social workers	37 (53.6)	16 (23.2)	14 (20.3)	14 (20.3)	17 (24.6)	32 (46.4)	16 (23.2)	24 (34.8)	29 (42.0)
Occupational therapists	18 (46.2)	11 (28.2)	9 (23.1)	7 (17.9)	8 (20.5)	19 (48.7)	5 (12.8)	8 (20.5)	25 (64.1)
Consultant psychiatrists	12 (63.2)	4 (21.1)	3 (15.8)	2 (10.5)	16 (84.2)	1 (5.3)	9 (47.4)	6 (31.6)	4 (21.1)
Doctors (other than consultants)	2 (18.2)	3 (27.3)	5 (45.5)	1 (9.1)	4 (36.4)	7 (63.6)	4 (36.4)	1 (9.1)	6 (54.5)
Community support workers	4 (36.4)	5 (45.5)	2 (18.2)	0 (0)	4 (36.4)	5 (45.5)	4 (36.4)	1 (9.1)	6 (54.5)
Clinical psychologists	14 (41.2)	9 (26.5)	10 (29.4)	4 (11.8)	5 (14.7)	24 (70.6)	7 (20.6)	8 (23.5)	19 (55.9)
Other specialist therapists	4 (57.1)	2 (28.6)	1 (14.3)	2 (28.6)	4 (57.1)	1 (14.3)	0 (0)	2 (28.6)	5 (71.4)
Administrative staff (including receptionists)	10 (24.4)	10 (24.4)	20 (48.8)	12 (29.3)	7 (17.1)	17 (41.5)	5 (12.2)	4 (9.8)	29 (70.7)
Volunteer staff	0 (0)	0 (0)	5 (100.0)	1 (20.0)	0 (0)	3 (60.0)	0 (0)	0 (0)	4 (80.0)
Others	6 (50.0)	1 (8.3)	2 (16.7)	2 (16.7)	3 (25.0)	4 (33.3)	3 (25.0)	3 (25.0)	5 (41.7)
WHOLE SAMPLE	197 (44.3)	109 (24.5)	126 (28.3)	59 (13.3)	83 (18.7)	262 (58.9)	82 (18.4)	104 (23.4)	245 (55.1)

NB. Cut off points based on the MBI mental health sub-group norms. Categorisation as "High" on personal accomplishment corresponds to low scores. Percentages base includes missing cases so do not always add up to 100%.

No comparable data for mental health services exist, but a study of NHS staff found more people taking sick leave for longer periods.[17] A tendency towards taking less sick leave may reflect increasing concern, particularly among nurses, over job security and the implications of a poor sickness record.[21]

Circumstances associated with job satisfaction and reduced burnout

The central question for policy is: 'What helps to produce positive outcomes for staff?' We began with an assumption that staff with high job satisfaction and low burnout would tend to be clear about the role of the team and their own personal role, and would identify with the team and their own profession or discipline[22]. We also assumed that they would have small caseloads, a small proportion of the caseload dedicated to people with severe and long-term mental health problems and low frequency of contact with service users.

Our attention to role ambiguity arises from the fact that it is often cited as a source of stress and job dissatisfaction.[23] It exists when a person is unclear about what is expected of his or her work and uncertain of the responses of others to his or her behaviour. It can be affected by aspects of the organisation in which a person works, such as the clarity of its aims and the way this is communicated by managers and supervisors.[24]

In CMHTs, role ambiguity may be made worse where the role of the team itself is unclear. This is a frequent criticism of CMHTs and CMHCs.[4, 5, 7] Moreover, the shift to community care may be a major source of role ambiguity in itself, as it often threatens longstanding attitudes and practices. As noted over ten years ago:

> 'The concept of community mental health calls for an unlearning of traditional patterns of professional interaction and of traditional conceptions of the nature of psychiatric disorders. Mental health workers are asked to break free of the historically grounded frameworks which have shaped their ideas, their respective professional **identities**, and the habits of their individual and collective work'[25]

Putting practitioners into teams places them in a special dilemma. They become members of two groups: their discipline and the team. As a result they may find themselves torn between the aims of a community mental health movement that explicitly values egalitarianism, role blurring and a surrender of power to lower-status workers and service users on the one hand, and a desire to hold on to traditional, socially-valued role definitions and practices on the other. It might, therefore, be predicted that the ideal conditions for team membership would be where a positive sense of belonging to the team can exist along side continued professional identification. This is most likely to occur when the discipline has a clear and valued role within the team, which in turn requires that the team itself has a clear role.

What did we find? Overall, team identification and team role clarity is associated with job satisfaction, but not burnout.[26] When staff who have both high identification with their team and with their profession are considered, however, they are found to have the highest job satisfaction and lowest burnout. The same is true of those team members who are clear about both the role of their team and their own role within it. See Appendix 1 for further details.[27]

Although team identification and team role clarity are correlated, further research is needed to establish whether clear service goals foster a positive sense of belonging to the service or vice versa.

Some of our results are particularly surprising, given our predictions. For instance, there is no association between job satisfaction or burnout and caseload size, caseload composition, frequency of contact with service users or the number of days that the team member worked with the team.[28] We return to the implications of these findings after considering some qualitative data.

Sources of reward

In order to understand better what makes for job satisfaction and reduced burnout, we asked those surveyed to describe the three 'most rewarding aspects' of their jobs and the three 'most difficult to tolerate sources of pressure'. We then classified the written responses using categories derived from the results.

Table 4 sets out the principal sources of reward, covering those features cited by ten per cent or more of those surveyed. It can be seen that over half (52%)

refer to aspects of working in a team or across disciplines. We view it as encouraging that so many found this to be a major source of satisfaction. The highly rewarding nature of clinical work is also evident; the second and and third categories both refer to this and, taken together, represent two thirds (66%) of those surveyed. Other key sources of satisfaction, it can be noted, include aspects of the job (29%) and power (25%).

Table 4 – Principal sources of reward

Source	Number of references	% of respondents
Team/multidisciplinary work	233	52
Being effective clinically	194	44
Clinical work generally	166	37
Aspects of the job itself	127	29
Power	110	25
Being effective as a service	76	17
Being valued	62	14
Rewards	58	13
Personal effectiveness	50	11

To provide more of the flavour of these issues, some direct quotations from team members are given below.

Team/multidisciplinary work
Most comments here described being in a team with supportive colleagues and working well together in a committed, cohesive and sometimes humorous way:

'Relationships with colleagues – mutual support, respect and fun.'
Consultant Psychiatrist, in a team based across three locations

'There is tremendous pressure in this job, but somehow you don't feel it because the atmosphere in the workplace is very relaxed and there is constant advice and support available.'
'Other' worker, based in the community, above theraputic workshop

'The atmosphere of the team is very supportive and open and we all share a slightly off-key sense of humour.'
Occupational Therapist, community resource centre

'Day to day camaraderie within the team.'
Consultant Psychiatrist, in-patient unit

'A good team sense of humour – which helps us rise above our difficulties to a certain extent.'
CPN, community resource centre

Being effective clinically

Most responses in this category noted positive outcomes for service users as a result of the team member's efforts:

'Seeing clients who would ordinarily have faced institutionalisation in the past functioning effectively in the community.'
CPN, community resource centre

'A great sense of achievement when the work I have done leads to a good outcome for the client.'
CPN, community mental health centre

Clinical work generally

This is a more general category, where staff described the rewards of contact with clients and their carers as well as work with particular client groups. Those who valued the variety of clients seen and their relationships with them are also included:

'Key working clients – getting to know them very well – especially finally getting their co-operation after months of refusal.'
Occupational Therapist, community resource centre

'Being remembered by people (clients) who haven't seen me for a considerable time.'
Student Psychiatric Nurse, community mental health centre

'I'm learning all the time from my patients to be more effective in understanding and treating mental illness.'
CPN, primary-care

'Working with clients who want to change and watching them achieve their goals.'
CPN, community mental health centre

'Patient contact (when workload controlled!)'
Consultant Psychiatrist, community mental health centre

Aspects of the job itself

The particular tasks or features of the working environment which are valued by team members are covered here. These include opportunities for innovation, variety, challenge and training. Particularly valued tasks included inter-agency work, group work, supervising others, project work and management. Some made particular mention of the benefits of community work:

'The broad range of life situations encountered in the client group.'
CPN, community mental health centre

'Supporting people in the community – not being divorced from the social realities.'
Nurse, community resource centre

'The team's continued commitment to in-service training – stops you going stale.'
CPN, residential care

'Not working in an institution.'
Nurse, community mental health centre

Power

Two thirds of these responses referred to autonomy. Others made reference to power, influence, status, responsibility and opportunities to participate in decision-making:

'Autonomy – being left to get on with the job, which happens rarely these days.'
CPN, community mental health centre

Being effective as a service

The rewards of the job also came from being part of a 'good' CMHT. This meant being capable of successful organisational change, providing a wide range of valued services and progressing together towards better practice:

'Seeing people who have had mental illness for a long time having a vastly improved quality of life, as a result of receiving a total service which looks at all aspects of their life.'
Consultant Psychiatrist, based in an office complex

Being valued

Roughly half these responses referred to being thanked by clients for work undertaken. It was also important for staff to feel valued and respected by colleagues, managers and those referring clients to them:

'Nice when occasionally (just occasionally) a patient says 'thanks!' for getting them better.'
Consultant Psychiatrist, community mental health centre

'The sense of respect I get from some colleagues who, though more 'qualified', acknowledge my experience and are willing to defer at times.'
Nurse in a team based in an in-patient unit

'The smile on people's faces – knowing you have played a part in their well-being – being thanked.'
Administrative worker, community mental health centre

'Being accepted as a team member and not just a nursing assistant. My opinion is often sought and acknowledged.'
Nursing Assistant, community mental health centre

Rewards

This general category covered specific personal outcomes as a result of work. There were only 21 references to pay. More mention was made of personal development, satisfaction and enjoyment:

'Making perceptible progress myself in learning alongside my patients.'
An information technology rehabilitation project co-ordinator, community mental health centre

Learning more about what 'makes me tick' as well.'
CPN, community resource centre

'I have gained confidence (being able to deal with difficult situations), and am hopefully more assertive.'
Administrative worker, primary care

Personal effectiveness

It was important for staff to feel they were making good use of their skills other than those used in clinical work. Some made general references to the rewards of 'getting the job done' and being effective in relationships with other staff:

'The relatively infrequent occasions when I am asked to use specifically psychological skills or other skills I have been trained in (e.g. research) – especially non-direct client work in the organisation.'
Clinical Psychologist, community mental health centre

Sources of pressure

Table 5 – Principal sources of pressure

Source	Number of references	% of respondents
Lack of resources	173	39
Work overload	158	36
Bureaucracy	137	31
Management	124	28
Managing competing tasks	80	18
Organisational change	75	17
Role problems	57	13
Interpersonal issues	55	12
Work with service users	54	12
Working conditions	50	11
Team problems	48	11

Table 5 sets out the most frequently cited sources of pressure. It can be seen that lack of resources heads the list (mentioned by nearly two fifths), followed by work overload, bureaucracy and management. It is notable that these were a concern to a far greater number of people than other predictable sources of pressure, such as working with challenging clients, problems in the team or working conditions.

Again, it may be useful to provide some flavour of the issues raised.

Lack of resources

Problems cited here included resources to do the job (such as training and supervision), lack of staff and an absence of services for people to refer on to, as well as insufficient funding.

'It is highly stressful to attempt to do a job properly without adequate alternative professions to refer to if you are not suitable. We find ourselves stuck with clients no one else will see, due to their own profession-specific selection processes.'
CPN, based in 'half a local council office'

Lack of development of CMHTs was often ascribed to resource constraints. A number of provider units were undergoing Trust status applications with associated changes in finance. A particular problem raised by funding constraints was difficulties in securing staff other than CPNs. Problems filling occupational therapy and psychology posts were particularly stressed. In some areas, financial constraints on the local authority had led to social workers not being replaced.

'As a result of social services reorganisation, there has been a drastic reduction of social work input to the team, which everyone recognises is very destructive and prevents the team from functioning efficiently. There is a feeling of powerlessness that decisions about staffing have been taken for political reasons without any consideration of the needs of users.'
Consultant Psychiatrist, based in an office complex

Work overload

Concern here tended to be focused on the sheer number of referrals, the size of caseloads and difficulties managing workload generally:

'Having to discharge people off my caseload too soon because of pressure of new referrals.'
CPN, community mental health centre

'Allocation meetings – justifying that you have no space on your caseload.'
CPN, community mental health centre

'Being pulled hard in two directions – GP referrals (income generating) and severe mental illness.'
CPN, community mental health centre

Bureaucracy

Paperwork was highlighted as a major problem, particularly where it concerned health and social care reforms. General 'red tape' and meetings were also cited:

'As well as written reports on all contacts with clients, there is an expectation that Comcare be completed in all cases... It is time consuming and rather coronary inducing. Time saved could be better used in having more contacts with clients.'
CPN, community mental health centre

'Change-over from working independently to working in a team requires many hours per week in meetings – referral meetings, operational policy meetings, team meetings and future time out for supervision/staff support meetings.'
Occupational Therapist, community mental health centre

Management

Managers were seen as lacking understanding, providing too few opportunities for participation in decision-making, communicating poorly or failing to provide management or leadership at all. Changing or ambiguous management structures were also noted:

'Management is out of touch with reality.'
CPN, community mental health centre

'Clinical directorate system...where psychologists are caught between clinical managers who want to own and control the psychologists and psychiatrists who want to be the gatekeepers of all mental health services.'
Clinical Psychologist without a team base

'Unclear lines of management, poor communication with senior managers. There appears to be a degree of conflict between line managers and service directors.'
CPN, community mental health centre

'Management issues cause confusion for team members, due to individual professions retaining their line-management accountability and organisational operational policies. This hampers joint working.'
Social Worker without a team base

Managing competing tasks

Staff noted both lack of time and difficulty managing the time that was available. For some, coping with unscheduled emergencies or statutory work was a particular source of stress:

'Several emergencies taking place in one day. Booked appointments then have to be re-arranged.'
Social Worker, community mental health centre

Organisational change

The major concern here was the radical changes in health and social care delivery.

'Changes instigated by central government, which I feel could destroy the model of working to which I subscribe – CMHTs.'
Social Worker, community mental health centre

It might be added here that organisational change was the most frequently raised topic under a request for general comments. Perhaps this is not surprising. Many health authorities are still in the process of developing CMHTs, often following changes to locality or sector-based services. Many teams appear to be working towards stronger management at team level, location on a single site, single access points for the receipt of referrals and increased user involvement. The Care Programme Approach has prompted multidisciplinary working in many areas, but not necessarily the development of CMHTs.

The role of general practitioners as purchasers also gave rise to concern. Staff feared that GPs would tend to contract with specific disciplines for provision, while remaining largely ignorant of the advantages of a team approach. GP fund-holding was also seen as a threat to sectorised services and therefore, to multidisciplinary teams aiming to provide services to people within a particular area. Some predicted that the greater purchasing role of GPs would shift demand for service provision towards those with less severe mental health problems.

Role problems

These tended to concern coping with multiple roles and demands, clarifying and communicating roles to others and particularly taking on new and ambiguous roles such as care management:

'Individuals who continue to see OTs as 'basket weavers'! Having almost to justify my existence to others (e.g. GPs) where other team members don't. I am equally skilled.'
Occupational Therapist, community resource centre

'Arguments over washing up coffee cups.'
Nurse in a team based across three locations

Interpersonal issues

Some reported that they had colleagues who were simply 'difficult to work with'. In addition, there were specific clashes of ideology and issues of inequality:

'Working in an office with a group of people who do not work as a team. The office is used as a work base, with each worker protecting their own wicket. There is no commitment to providing a client-centred service.'
Social Worker without a shared team base

'Being treated as less than equal by certain team members because of my age, sex and profession.'
Administrative worker, community mental health centre

Work with service users

Work with very distressed or difficult clients was highlighted, along with concerns over client expectations:

'Dealing with feelings/emotions related to clients 'in crisis', e.g. clients who are suicidal due to bereavement.'
Occupational Therapist, community mental health centre

Working conditions

These can often be a source of problems. Here, particular concern was raised about the implications of job insecurity and poor pay:

31

'I'm always under threat of redundancy these days, which makes it difficult to complain about caseload numbers, etc.'
CPN without a shared base

'Veiled threats which make me feel insecure, e.g. re-profiling (which is about cheap labour and I'm expensive).'
Nurse, community mental health centre

Team problems

Problems within the team included poor communication, lack of leadership and unclear team goals.

'Trying to agree/implement change within a multidisciplinary team context is like trying to coax an elephant up a mountain.'
Clinical Psychologist, community mental health centre

'Unclear expectations as to the purpose of my clients' expressed needs, versus professionally-assessed needs.'
Occupational Therapist, community resource centre

'A feeling that systems within the team perpetuate themselves, rather than serve the needs of clients.'
Social Worker, community mental health centre

Other problems

It is notable that less than one tenth of team members made reference to inter-agency problems, concern over being controlled from outside the team (particularly pressure to be resource rather than needs-led), inter-disciplinary differences, conflict with their own profession or concerns intrinsic to the personality of the worker.

Conclusions on the sources of job satisfaction and burnout

Both the qualitative and quantitative data point to the importance of team factors in predicting job satisfaction among team members. Positive relationships with team members appear to be a major source of reward and may contribute to the widely reported positive identification with the team. Clarity about the role of the team also appears to be important in achieving this positive identification and to being clear about one's own role in the team.

We note with interest that working with people with severe and long-term mental health problems may not be as stressful as would be predicted from earlier research[29]. Indeed, it can be a major source of reward, particularly where staff feel effective in their work. It is, therefore, not surprising that lack of resources is so frequently identified as a source of pressure. In order to be and feel effective, staff obviously need adequate resources.

Bureaucracy (particularly paperwork) and problems in relating to management also emerge as major sources of pressure. This may bear on the absence of clear strategic management, highlighted above, and the failure of operational managers to communicate the rationale for new procedures and organisational change.

We might add that it is likely that team members used our postal survey to some extent as a medium for complaint, rather than as an authentic report of experience. Even if we interpret the data in this way, it is important that their concerns are acknowledged and responded to.

The Individual Disciplines

It is essential in such discussions not to blur important differences across the disciplines. In particular, how do they differ in their work and their experience of being in the team? We found differences on all measures of burnout (see Table 3) and job satisfaction (see Figure 3), the extent of clarity about the role of the team and their personal role within it, and professional identification. These are summarised for each discipline below. Some differences between disciplines in caseload size, caseload composition and the frequency with which service users are seen are shown in Appendix 1.

Community psychiatric nurses
CPNs are the largest staff group within CMHTs. Of all the disciplines, they devote most time to the team (a mean of 4.6 days per week) and have spent most time working in mental health.

Aside from doctors, CPNs have the largest caseloads (mean=34 individuals) and see most of their clients fortnightly or more often.

However, people with severe and long-term mental health problems make up less than half of their caseloads on average. This is of considerable concern, particularly in view of the imperative from the recent *Mental Health Nursing Review* to target this client group.[30]

It is striking that nearly half (45%) of CPNs fall into our 'high emotional exhaustion' category. They are also among the least satisfied disciplines, particularly with respect to work relationships. Nonetheless, their sense of professional identification appears fairly strong and they most often have a combination of high team identification and professional identification and a clarity about the role of the team and their role within it.

Other nurses

Nurses other than CPNs are concentrated in CMHCs, day hospitals or centres and in teams not based together. They have a larger proportion of people with severe and long-term mental health problems on their caseloads than CPNs (62%, compared to 48%). Overall, however, they have very similar responses regarding job satisfaction, burnout, role clarity and team and professional identification.

Social workers

Social workers do not have particularly large caseloads, nor do they work with a large proportion of people with severe and long-term mental health problems. They see their clients significantly less often than support workers or CPNs.

Yet over half (54%) of the social workers are highly exhausted emotionally. Compared with other disciplines, they also have a comparatively low sense of personal accomplishment and a high degree of depersonalisation. They also have the least satisfaction with work relationships and least overall job satisfaction.

It is important to consider why social workers fare so badly. The answer may lie in confusion about their jobs and their place in the team. Despite being second only to nurses in the amount of time dedicated per week to their CMHT, they tend to be comparatively unclear about the role of the team and their role within it. They also tend to have low identification with their team and profession. Indeed, of all disciplines they have the least positive sense of belonging to their profession.

It may also be that the recent introduction of care management has created considerable confusion among social workers with respect to their own roles as purchasers or providers, and the roles of colleagues in the team. Clearly, social workers require urgent support and guidance to resolve these complex issues if their invaluable role in helping to ensure continuous and co-ordinated social care provision is not to be squandered. Reconciling the Care Programme Approach and care management through joint health and social services models of care management may offer a positive way forward.[10,31]

Psychiatrists

Consultant psychiatrists ostensibly have the largest caseloads of any group surveyed, although we believe that these may include all those people for whom they are medically responsible. This fact may explain the additional finding that they see the smallest proportion of their caseloads fortnightly or more frequently. On average, roughly two thirds (63%) of their caseloads comprise people with severe and long-term mental health problems. As noted above, their involvement in CMHTs is comparatively limited, which may be detrimental to providing comprehensive and high quality care.

We found that consultant psychiatrists are the most emotionally exhausted and have the greatest sense of depersonalisation of any discipline. 12 of the 19 sampled fall into the 'high' emotional exhaustion category.

There is some anecdotal evidence that psychiatrists in CMHTs are vulnerable to burnout because they see themselves as having 'a lot of responsibility but not the corresponding authority'.[32] Issues of accountability and responsibility are frequently a source of contention and confusion within teams. Doctors often have an enduring sense of overall responsibility for the work of the team as a whole, even though this is not supported by Government guidance or case law.[33] Definitive clarification of these ambiguities is long overdue and is all the more pressing because of the planned introduction of supervised discharge, which provides psychiatrists with special new powers.

In contrast to the other disciplines, the proportion of consultant psychiatrists experiencing a sense of depersonalisation is significantly higher than the scale norms for mental health staff. Nine of the 19 consultants sampled fell into the 'high depersonalisation' category. This may be because their large caseloads of people seen comparatively infrequently mean that they have less opportunity to develop positive personal relationships with service users. We have noted that contact with service users is a major source of reward for practitioners. If psychiatrists are not benefiting from this contact, they may be denied an important buffer against burnout.

Despite these problems, consultant psychiatrists report the highest satisfaction with work relationships and very high job satisfaction overall. The pattern of job satisfaction in our data, broadly paralleling hierarchical status, is typical of other studies[34], particularly concerning satisfaction with achievement, value and growth. It may be that variations in salary are a concrete factor in making staff feel more valued. Consultant psychiatrists also have a high sense of personal accomplishment, second only to voluntary staff.

Consultant psychiatrists are notable in reporting the highest level of positive identification with their team and the greatest clarity about their personal roles. The majority of consultant psychiatrists also report being clear about the role of the team.

It was not possible to ascertain the grade of the 11 non-consultant doctors in this study, with the exception of two senior house officers. Like consultants, these other doctors have large caseloads, but with a smaller proportion of people with severe and long-term mental health problems. In general, they share the consultants' high job satisfaction, but are less emotionally exhausted and report less depersonalisation. This may be because they feel less responsible for the service and its clients.

With shifts towards community care and an increase in operational management at team level, disciplines within CMHTs are likely to become increasingly autonomous and less likely to accept that psychiatrists should assume an overall leadership role. There is a danger that psychiatrists will feel devalued by such a change and, in consequence, they may opt out of CMHT work and their invaluable contribution will be lost.

Psychiatrists are essential to ensuring continuity of medical management when service users are admitted to in-patient beds and when liaising with primary care. As definitions of their responsibilities become clearer, psychiatrists may emerge with a narrower, more medically focused, consulting role (akin to that often found in services for people with learning disabilities). Whatever the outcome, when developing CMHTs it is important that their central role is appropriately acknowledged and rewarded.

Clinical psychologists

Despite having comparatively small caseloads, with small proportions of people with severe and long-term mental health problems, clinical psychologists are among the most emotionally exhausted disciplines. They also have comparatively low satisfaction with work relationships. On the other hand, they have high satisfaction with achievement, value and growth, perhaps because of their relatively high status and autonomy. For example, the survey identified teams where referrals had to be made to a single point, except when referring to medical staff or clinical psychologists.

Clinical psychologists are unique among professions in reporting comparatively low team identification, but high professional identification. They also have low personal and team role clarity. Their professional literature suggests that clinical psychologists feel their professional identification to be particularly threatened by team membership.[35]

Occupational therapists

Occupational therapists have comparatively small caseloads of which, on average, slightly less than half (45%) consists of people with severe and long-term mental health problems. Aside from nurses, they are the only profession dedicating, on average, four days a week or more to the team.

They report only moderate levels of emotional exhaustion and personal accomplishment, with a very low sense of depersonalisation. They have comparatively high job satisfaction regarding achievement, value and growth, satisfaction with work relationships and strong team identification. Their lack of professional identification, however, is second only to social workers. The largest proportion fall into the high team identification – low professional identification category. Most are clear about the role of the team and their own role within it.

The presence of occupational therapists is strongly associated with activities of particular relevance to people with severe and long-term mental health problems, such as training in activities of daily living and assisting clients in achieving satisfying work and leisure. Given that they also have comparatively low burnout and strong team commitment, occupational therapists may offer the best model for professional input to CMHTs currently available.

Community support workers

Community support workers are among the youngest and least experienced team members. They carry small caseloads (mean=13 individuals), with the largest proportion of people with severe and long-term mental health problems (84%). Most (88%) of their caseload is seen at least fortnightly.

It is notable that despite frequent contact with people with severe and long-term mental health problems, community support workers do not report high levels of burnout, although their sense of depersonalisation is high compared to other disciplines. They do, however, have comparatively low job satisfaction, particularly with achievement, value and growth, and work relations. This may reflect feelings of being devalued and isolated. Only volunteers report lower identification with the team. They have low professional identification and their personal role ambiguity is second only to clinical psychologists.

Given the acknowledged importance of community support workers in work with people with severe and long-term mental health problems, it is essential to ensure that their work is fully integrated into the work of the CMHT as a whole, in order to prevent their isolation. It is also crucial that the importance of their role is properly acknowledged through adequate training and pay.

Administrative staff

The role of administrative staff in CMHTs is often neglected. As they contribute the most input per week to CMHTs, they may provide invaluable continuity of communication and co-ordination of team operations, particularly when teams are otherwise fairly fragmented. Effective administrative co-ordination may be particularly important in complex multidisciplinary, multi-agency work. Adequate administrative support was recently reported as critical to the success or failure of attempts to implement the Care Programme Approach.[36] It is worrying that some CMHTs (15%) appear to have no administrative staff at all.

Administrative staff have a strong sense of team identification and are clear about their own roles and the role of the team. They have the lowest sense of personal accomplishment, however, and comparatively low job satisfaction except concerning work relationships.

4 Conclusions and Recommendations

It is clear that the transition from mainly in-patient care to community care has not been a smooth one. Those working in mental health care find themselves in a very different environment from that which they were trained for, and which they are used to.

This research underlines that changes need to be made both now and in the longer term. The Sainsbury Centre for Mental Health believes that a major reappraisal of professional roles, pre- and post-qualification training, and management structures is well overdue. The key findings of this project indicate that there are a number of steps which need to be taken now, if community mental health teams are to be effective, and if dedicated and valuable staff are to be retained within the field.

1. **Overall, staff are emotionally over-extended and exhausted. Nurses, social workers, consultant psychiatrists and clinical psychologists are particularly affected. Lack of resources is a major source of pressure and feeling able to work effectively with service users is a major source of reward.**

   Purchasers and senior managers need to ensure that adequate resources are available for staff to perform their roles effectively.

2. **Job satisfaction and burnout are not strongly associated with caseload size, composition or the frequency of client contacts. However, excessively large caseloads of people seen infrequently, as in the case of consultant psychiatrists, may result in poorer quality relationships with service users.**

   Staff roles should be designed to promote good quality, long-term relationships with service users through establishing realistic clinical demands and caseloads.

3. **Consultant psychiatrists are particularly vulnerable to emotional exhaustion and the development of negative and unfeeling**

attitudes towards service users. This may reflect both their large caseloads of people seen comparatively infrequently and their enduring sense of being responsible for the work of the service as a whole.

The size of consultant psychiatrist caseloads should be reviewed and the definition of 'medical responsibility' within CMHTs clarified.

4. **On average, people with severe and long-term mental health problems make up less than half of a CPN's caseload.**

    Purchasers, general managers and senior nurse managers need to provide CPNs with adequate incentives, training and support if they are to work effectively with people with severe and long-term mental health problems. Their training should include providing psycho-social interventions which are established as being effective for this client group.[37]

5. **Social workers generally are more burnt out and less satisfied with their jobs than other disciplines. They are particularly unclear about the role of the team and their own role within it and have low levels of identification with their team and with their profession. This confusion may have been exacerbated by the introduction of care management.**

    Health and social services authorities need to ensure that the roles of social workers are clearly defined within local arrangements for care management and the Care Programme Approach.

6. **Community support workers are generally young and inexperienced, whilst working almost exclusively with people with severe and long-term mental health problems. They have comparatively low job satisfaction and little sense of positive team membership.**

    Attention should be given to examining the role of community support workers and integrating their work with the rest of the CMHT, to ensure that they feel appropriately valued. The role of community support workers in teams is the subject of a new Sainsbury Centre for Mental Health study.

7. **Fragmented teams, with considerable part-time input, are less likely to have a large proportion of people with severe and long-term mental health problems on their caseloads.**

More full-time commitment to CMHTs is required.

8. **CMHTs are still most often based in community mental health centres. There is evidence that such teams do not place enough emphasis on people with severe and long-term mental health problems.**

Purchasers and senior managers need to be more critical about the need to provide a team base where services are provided. Investing in staff who can take services to where they are needed may be a more effective alternative.

9. **Teams based in primary-care settings have the smallest proportion of people with severe and long-term mental health problems on their caseloads.**

Although it is clearly important to have good links between CMHTs and primary health care teams, CMHTs should not be based in primary-care settings if they are to prioritise people with severe and long-term mental health problems. This may help them to gate-keep referrals.

10. **Teams providing the first contact point for all mental health referrals in a locality have a significantly lower proportion of people with severe and long-term mental health problems on their caseloads. This may represent greater pressure from GPs and primary health care teams to accept people with less severe mental health problems.**

CMHTs should be clear about their priority client groups. Eligibility criteria should be widely publicised and systems for gate-keeping referrals established. In particular, priorities should be agreed with primary health care teams. Caseload mix should be regularly monitored.

11. **The provision of practical psycho-social interventions is associated with teams focusing on people with severe and long-term mental health problems.**

43

If CMHTs are to focus on people with severe and long-term mental health problems, purchasers and senior managers must ensure that an appropriate skill-mix is available within or via the CMHT to deliver the required range of relevant services. Those professional disciplines which see themselves taking a major role in the provision of community-based care for this client group, need to be clear about the relevance of their skills to the work of CMHTs.

12. **Less than a quarter of CMHTs currently provide access to users out-of-hours or at weekends.**

Purchasers, CMHT staff and their managers should develop ways of extending support for service users beyond 9 am to 5 pm, Monday to Friday.

13. **Many teams have included the tasks required under care management within the existing responsibilities carried out by professional team members.**

Health and social services purchasers and senior managers should be responsible for ensuring that duplication and conflict among those assessing, purchasing and co-ordinating health and social care. Joint care management models, where health and social services staff share a 'core' care management role, should be adopted.

14. **Although most teams have direct access to hospital beds via medical team members, less than one third of teams retain responsibility for planning care following admission.**

In-patient beds should be a resource that CMHTs can use flexibly when required. Continuity of planning and provision is required throughout in-patient stays. Beds should be attached to sectorised teams and control of them transferred to community-based medical staff.

15. **Increasingly, CMHTs have team managers or co-ordinators. Despite this, responsibility for key strategic and operational management tasks remains dispersed or ill-defined.**

Purchasers and general managers need to ensure that CMHTs have clear remits concerning client group and operation. Each team should have a manager, who has clear operational management responsibilities over all the disciplines involved.

16. **Practitioners who are clear both about their team's role and their own roles have lower burnout and higher job satisfaction. They also have stronger identification with the team than those who are unclear about its role.**

In order to promote job satisfaction and reduce burnout, CMHTs should promote a positive sense of group membership that boosts self-esteem without creating personal role ambiguity. This requires that team development takes due account of (a) valuing the team and its staff through adequate pay, public support and acknowledgment, training and other resources, and (b) ensuring that roles within the team are clearly defined and appropriately and unambiguously managed.

17. **There is a considerable ambiguity about the allocation of operational and clinical management responsibilities within teams.**

General managers and professional line managers should make it clear to each team member who they are accountable to and for which responsibilities.

18. **Genuine user participation in CMHTs remains comparatively undeveloped.**

Purchasers, senior managers, CMHT members and service users need to devote time and resources to informing themselves about effective models of user participation and ensuring that these are realised in practice.

19. **Organisational change, uncertainty and poor management are significant sources of pressure for staff.**

Managers need to acknowledge and respond to the effects of change on staff by keeping them as informed as possible, promoting participation in management decisions and responding to concerns.

Working with people with severe and long-term mental health problems tends to lack the 'cachet' of primary-care, preventive work or dynamic psychotherapy and has long been the 'Cinderella' of mental health services. Fortunately, the needs of people with severe and long-term mental health problems are being repeatedly underlined as deserving priority.[38]

Mental health services are in a period of great upheaval and organisational change, during which staff need clear leadership and management. This, in turn, requires effective collaboration between health commissioners, GP fund-holders and purchasers in social services, to define responsibilities at all levels.

Clearly, those currently working in community mental health services value their jobs and find great rewards in their work with service users. Given strong leadership, good management, clear and appropriate roles within the team, relevant training and the resources they need to do their jobs well, these individuals will be equipped to provide people with severe and long-term mental health problems with the services they need.

As a result, working within CMHTs would become a more valued activity, undertaken by more valued staff. This will increase the status of comparatively low-status staff such as support workers, while attracting further time from practitioners who already enjoy high status. With this wide and co-ordinated skill mix in place, working in the 'Cinderella service' may yet be a ball!

Endnotes

1. Onyett, S., Heppleston, T. and Bushnell, D. (1994) *The Organisation and Operation of Community Mental Health Teams in England: A national survey*. London: The Sainsbury Centre for Mental Health.

2. Ovretveit, J. (1993) *Coordinating Community Care: Multidisciplinary teams and care management*. Buckingham: Open University Press.

3. Knapp, M., Cambridge, P., Thomason, C., Allen, C., Beecham, J. and Darton, R. (1992) *Care in the Community: Challenge and Demonstration*. Aldershot: Gower.

   Merson, S., Tyrer, P., Onyett, S., Lack, S., Birkett, P., Lynch, S. and Johnson, T. (1992) 'Early intervention in psychiatric emergencies: a controlled clinical trial'. *The Lancet*, 339, 1311 – 1314.

   Marks, I. M., Connolly, J., Muijen, M., Audini, B., McNamee, G. and Lawrence, R. E. (1994) 'Home-based versus hospital-based care for people with serious mental illnesses'. *British Journal of Psychiatry*, 165, 179 – 194.

4. Sayce, L., Craig, T. K. J. and Boardman, A. P. (1991) 'The development of community mental health centres in the UK'. *Social Psychiatry and Psychiatric Epidemiology*, 26: 14 – 20.

5. Peck, E. (1994) 'Community mental health centres: challenges to the new orthodoxy'. *Journal of Mental Health*, 3, 151 – 156.

6. 'Severe' was defined for this study as a level of distress or disturbance that could normally result in a diagnosis of psychosis, psychiatric admission or community-based interventions to prevent admission. 'Long term' was defined as intense service use (e.g. hospital admissions or weekly home visits) over six months or more. People suffering from organic illness, brain injury or extreme personal trauma were included.

7. Patmore, C. and Weaver, T. (1991) *Community Mental Health Teams: Lessons for planners and managers.* London: Good Practices in Mental Health.

8. Shepherd, G., Murray, A., and Muijen, M. (1994) *Relative Values. The differing views of users, family carers and professionals on services for people with schizophrenia in the community.* London: The Sainsbury Centre for Mental Health.

9. Ritchie, J. Dick, D. and Lingham, R. (1994) *Report of the Inquiry into the Care and Treatment of Christopher Clunis.* London. HMSO.

10. Department of Health (1994) *Draft Guide to Arrangements for Inter-agency Working for the Care and Protection of Severely Mentally Ill People.* Issued for consultation on 10th October 1994.

11. Warner, R. (1985) *Recovery from Schizophrenia.* Boston: Routledge and Kegan Paul.

12. For a review of this literature see Onyett, S. R. (1992) *Case Management in Mental Health.* London: Chapman and Hall.

13. Jackson, G., Gater, R., Goldberg, D., Tantam, D., Loftus, L. and Taylor, H. (1993) 'A new community mental health team based in primary care'. *British Journal of Psychiatry*, 162, 375 – 384.

14. This was measured as the as the ratio of total full-time equivalents to people per team.

15. This was undertaken by dividing the full-time equivalent of each discipline by the number of people in that discipline for each team. Further details are provided in the earlier Sainsbury Centre report on this research.

16. Measured using the Occupational Stress Indicator. Cooper, C. L., Sloan, S, J. and Williams, S. (1988) *Occupational Stress Indicator Management Guide.* NFER-Nelson: Windsor.

17. Rees, D. and Cooper, C. (1992) 'Occupational stress in health service workers in the UK'. *Stress Medicine*, 8, 79 – 90.

18. Burnout in this study was measured using the *Maslach Burnout Inventory* (2nd edition) Maslach, C. and Jackson, S. E. 1986. Oxford Psychologists Press.

19. The inter-correlations between burnout and job satisfaction measures are given below. All are significant at p<0.001 but are generally low.

Emotional exhaustion – personal accomplishment	r = -0.17
Emotional exhaustion – depersonalisation.	r = 0.46
Emotional exhaustion – total job satisfaction.	r = -0.43
Personal accomplishment – depersonalisation.	r = -0.21
Personal accomplishment – total job satisfaction.	r = 0.27
Depersonalisation – total job satisfaction.	r = -0.23

20. Tested using the Z-statistic in a standard hypothesis text comparing mean scores with the MBI mental health subgroup (N=730). All differences are significant at p<0.01.

21. Seccombe, I., Ball, J. and Patch, A. (1993) *The Price of Commitment; Nurses' Pay, Careers and Prospects, 1993*. Report No. 251. Institute of Manpower Studies.

    UNISON (1994) *Caring Against the Odds*. London. UNISON

22. If respondents did not feel themselves to belong to a profession they were asked to consider the 'group of people who have had the same training as you or who would go under the same name'.

23. Rushton, A. (1987) 'Stress amongst social workers'. In. Payne, R. and Firth-Cozens, J. (Eds). *Stress in Health Professionals*. Chichester: Wiley.

24. Revicki, D. A. and May, H. J. (1989) 'Organizational characteristics, occupational stress and mental health in nurses'. *Behavioural Medicine*, 15(1), 30 – 36.

49

25. Lang, C. L. (1982) 'The resolution of status and ideological conflicts in a community mental health setting'. *Psychiatry, 45,* 159 – 171. (Quote from p.160)

26. The criteria used for an 'association' in this context was a 'modest' correlation of 0.4 or larger (after Cohen, L. and Holliday, M. (1992) *Statistics for Social Scientists.* London: Harper and Row). There was a correlation of -0.38 between emotional exhaustion and team role clarity.

27. With the four variables of team role clarity, personal role clarity, professional identification and team identification, 'high' and 'low' levels were determined using a median split for each. The proportion of each discipline falling into each of the four categories created for each variable is shown in Appendix 1.

28. The only inter-correlations between these measures was a low negative correlation between the size of caseloads and the proportion of caseload that was seen fortnightly or more (r=-0.31, p<0.001) and a low positive correlation between the proportion seen fortnightly or more and the proportion consisting of people with severe and long-term mental health problems (r=0.15, p<0.005).

29. Pines, A. and Maslach, C. (1978) 'Characteristics of staff burnout in mental health settings'. *Hospital and Community Psychiatry, 29(4),* 233 – 237.

    Oberlander, L. B. (1990) 'Work satisfaction among community-based mental health service providers: The association between work environment and work satisfaction'. *Community Mental Health Journal,* 26(6), 517 – 532.

30. Mental Health Nursing Review Team (1994) *Working in Partnership: A collaborative approach to care.* London. HMSO.

31. Onyett, S. R. and Davenport, S. (1994) 'Care programming and care management in Rochester'. *Community Care Management and Planning,* 1 (4), 116 – 123

32. Clarke, G.H. , and Vaccaro, J. V. (1987) 'Burnout among CMHC psychiatrists and the struggle to survive'. *Hospital and Community Psychiatry*, 38(8), 843 – 847.

33. British Psychological Society (1986) *Responsibility Issues in Clinical Psychology and Multidisciplinary Teamwork*. BPS. Leicester. This guidance is about to be up-dated but there is no new case law to substantially alter its conclusions or the Nodder report from which it draws many of its conclusions.

   Onyett, S. R. (in press). 'Responsibility and accountability in community mental health teams'. *Psychiatric Bulletin*.

34. Rees, and Cooper, (1992) *Op.cit* Only general managers recorded higher job satisfaction than doctors in this study.

35. Searle, R. T. (1991) 'Community mental health teams: fact or fiction'. *Clinical Psychology Forum*, 31, 15 – 17.

   Anciano, D. and Kirkpatrick, A. (1990) 'CMHTs and clinical psychology: the death of a profession?' *Clinical Psychology Forum*, 26, 9 – 12.

36. North, C. and Ritchie, J. (1993) *Factors Influencing the Implementation of the Care Programme Approach*. London: HMSO.

37. See for example, Brooker, C., Falloon, I., Butterworth, A., Goldberg, D., Graham-Hole, V. and Hillier, V. (1994) 'The outcome of training community psychiatric nurses to deliver psychosocial intervention'. *British Journal of Psychiatry*, 165, 222 – 230.

38. See for example, Mental Health Foundation (1994), *Creating Community Care*. London: Mental Health Foundation and Mental Health Nursing Review Team. (1994) *Working in Partnership: A collaborative approach to care*. London. HMSO.

Appendix 1

Correlation matrix of dependent and independent variables

	Team role clarity	Personal role clarity	Team identification	Professional identification	Case load size	% seen fortnightly or more	% severe and long-term mental health problems
Emotional exhaustion	-0.38*	-0.27*	-0.21*	0.06	0.01	0.04
Personal accomplishment	0.21*	0.17*	0.19*	0.27*	0.08	0.02
Depersonalisation	-0.26*	-0.19*	-0.18*	0.19*	-0.09	0.08
Total job satisfaction	0.51*	0.37*	0.51*	0.26*	0.06	0.10	-0.05	0.06
Achievement value and growth	0.36*	0.26*	0.34*	0.28*	0.08	-0.05	0.05
Organisational design	0.51*	0.35*	0.50*	0.12	0.10	-0.03	0.09
Job relations	0.54*	0.32*	0.61*	0.18*	0.12	-0.05	0.06
Sick leave	-0.08	-0.06	-0.07	-0.03	0.00	-0.01	0.00

N.B. * p<0.001. Only correlation greater than 0.40 are interpreted in the text.

Main effects and multiple comparisons

Main effects	Test statistic	Significance	Significant differences among multiple comparisons
Emotional exhaustion	$F_{(11,420)} = 2.9$	0.001	Cons > Vols, SWs > Vols, Admin.
Personal accomplishment	K-W $x^2 = 32.1$	0.001	CPNs > Admin.
Depersonalisation	K-W $x^2 = 42.5$	0.0001	Cons > CPNs, Admin.
Job satisfaction – Total	$F_{(11,375)} = 2.5$	0.01	SWs < Cons, OTs.
Job sat – Achievement value and growth	$F_{(11,414)} = 3.5$	0.0001	Cons > Supports, Admin, SWs, Other docs > Admin.
Job sat – Work relations	$F_{(11,409)} = 3.1$	0.001	Cons > SWs, CPNs. Admin > SWs.
Job sat – Organisational design	K-W $x^2 = 21.2$	0.05	None sig.
Team role clarity	$F_{(11,420)} = 2.8$	0.005	Admin > Psychols, SWs. about CPNs > SWs
Personal role clarity	$F_{(11,430)} = 3.0$	0.001	Cons, Admin > Psychols. Admin > SWs.
Team identification	K-W $x^2 = 20.8$	0.05	None sig.
Professional identification	K-W $x^2 = 37.9$	0.0001	CPNs > SWs, OTs.
Proportion of caseload with severe and long-term mental health problems	$F_{(10,366)} = 3.5$	0.001	Supports > CPNs, other docs, psychols, OTs, Vols.
Proportion of caseload seen fortnightly or more often	K-W $x^2 = 112.0$	0.0001	Cons < all others bar other docs. Supports > SWs, other docs. Vols > CPNs. Other nurses > CPNs, SWs, other docs. Psychols > Other docs. CPNs > SWs, Other docs.
Caseload size	K-W $x^2 = 87.0$	0.0001	Cons > CPNs, Other nurses, SWs, Psychols. CPNs > Psychols, OTs, Supports, Vols.
Days worked with team	K-W $x^2 = 112.1$	0.0001	CPNs > Cons, Other docs, Psychols, OTs, Vols. Other nurses > Cons, Other doctors, Psychols, Vols. SWs > Cons, Other docs. Admin staff > Cons, Other docs, Psychols, Vols.
Age	K-W $x^2 = 39.6$	0.0001	Support < SWs, Cons
Time worked in mental health	K-W $x^2 = 159.4$	0.0001	CPNs > all except Cons, Other nurses, Psychols. Other theraps. Cons > Supports, SWs, Other docs, Admin, Vols, Others, Psychols, Other theraps > Other docs. Other theraps > Other docs. Other nurses > Admin.

Key: Cons – consultant psychiatrists, SWs – social workers, Admin–admin staff (excluded from caseload analysis), Vols – volunteers, OTs – Occupational therapists, Psychols – Clinical psychologists, Supports – generic/community support workers, Other docs – doctors (other than consultants), Other nurses – nurses (other than CPNs), Other theraps – other specialist therapists.

Means (95% confidence intervals) for practice variables by discipline

Discipline	% of caseload with severe and long-term mental health problems	Caseload size	% of caseload seen fortnightly or more than once a fortnight	Days per week worked with the team
Community psychiatric nurses	48 (43 to 54)	34 (31 to 37)	62 (58 to 66)	4.6 (4.4 to 4.7)
Nurses (other than CPNs)	62 (48 to 76)	27 (19 to 35)	80 (71 to 90)	4.4 (3.9 to 4.8)
Social workers	55 (48 to 63)	27 (22 to 31)	49 (42 to 56)	4.2 (3.9 to 4.5)
Occupational therapists	45 (32 to 58)	22 (17 to 27)	61 (53 to 70)	3.9 (3.5 to 4.3)
Consultant psychiatrists	63 (48 to 78)	97 (58 to 136)	9 (5 to 13)	2.7 (2.2 to 3.1)
Doctors (other than consultants)	29 (14 to 44)	52 (20 to 84)	24 (8 to 40)	2.3 (1.5 to 3.1)
Generic mental health workers or support worker	84 (67 to 101)	13 (7 to 19)	88 (76 to 99)	4.1 (3.2 to 5.1)
Clinical psychologists	39 (27 to 52)	24 (17 to 30)	64 (54 to 73)	3.2 (2.7 to 3.7)
Other specialist therapists	36 (-9 to 82)	19 (1 to 37)	81 (62 to 100)	2.8 (0.9 to 4.7)
Administrative staff (including receptionists)	—	—	—	4.6 (4.3 to 5.0)
Volunteer staff	15 (-11 to 41)	4 (2 to 7)	100 (99 to 100)	1.5 (0.9 to 2.1)
Others	74 (40 to 107)	27 (5 to 48)	59 (31 to 87)	4.3 (3.4 to 5.3)
WHOLE SAMPLE	50 (47 to 54)	32 (29 to 35)	59 (56 to 62)	4.1 (4.0 to 4.3)

Significant differences between groups coded as high or low on team role clarity (TC) and personal role clarity (PC)

Outcome variable	Test statistic*	Multiple comparisons
Total job satisfaction	$F_{(3,371)} = 26.7$	High TC-high PC > all others. High TC-low PC > Low TC-low PC
Achievement, value and growth	$F_{(3,409)} = 15.6$	High TC-high PC > all others
Organisational design	$F_{(3,414)} = 26.4$	High TC-high PC > all others. High TC-low PC > Low TC-low PC
Work relations	$F_{(3,405)} = 27.2$	High TC-high PC > Low TC-high PC, Low TC-low PC. High TC-low PC > Low TC-low PC.
Emotional exhaustion	$F_{(3,415)} = 14.7$	High TC-high PC < Low TC-high PC, Low TC-low PC. High TC-low PC < Low TC-low PC
Personal accomplishment	$F_{(3,401)} = 7.4$	High TC-high PC > all others
Depersonalisation	KW $x^2 = 22.9$	High TC-high PC < all others. High TC-low PC < Low TC-low PC

*All significant at p<0.0001. Group sizes: High TC-high PC=175, High TC-low PC=64, Low TC-high PC=52, Low TC-low PC=139.

Significant differences between groups coded as high or low on team identification (TI) and professional identification (PI)

Outcome variable	Test statistic*	Multiple comparisons
Total job satisfaction	$F_{(3,364)} = 33.1$	High TI-high PI > all others. High TI-low PI > Low TI-high PI, Low TI-low PI Low TI-high PI > Low TI-low PI
Achievement, value and growth	$F_{(3,400)} = 20.7$	High TI-high PI > all others Low TI-low PI < all others
Organisational design	$F_{(3,405)} = 28.7$	High TI-high PI > Low TI-high PI, Low TI-low PI High TI-low PI > Low TI-high PI, Low TI-low PI
Work relations	$F_{(3,392)} = 44.7$	High TI-high PI > Low TI-high PI, Low TI-low PI, High TI-low PI > Low TI-high PI, Low TI-low PI
Emotional exhaustion	$F_{(3,403)} = 12.0$	High TI-high PI > all other
Personal accomplishment	$F_{(3,391)} = 7.0$	Low TI-low PI < all others
Depersonalisation	$KW\ x^2 = 21.8$	High TI-high PI > High TI-low PI, Low TI-low PI

*All significant at p<0.0001. Group sizes: High TI-high PI=132, High TI-low PI=87, Low TI-high PI=86, Low TI-low PI=113.

Percentage distribution of disciplines in high and low team (TC) and personal role clarity (PC) categories

Discipline	High TC – High PC	High TC – Low PC	Low TC – High PC	Low TC – Low PC
Community psychiatric nurses	43.8	14.2	13.0	29.0
Nurses (other than CPNs)	46.7	10.0	6.7	36.7
Social workers	25.4	11.9	13.4	49.3
Occupational therapists	41.7	16.7	5.6	36.1
Consultant psychiatrists	58.8	11.8	17.6	11.8
Clinical psychologists	23.5	20.6	11.8	44.1
Administrative staff (including receptionists)	56.4	17.9	15.4	10.3
WHOLE SAMPLE	40.7	14.9	12.1	32.3

Percentage distribution of disciplines in high and low team (TI) and professional identification (PI) categories

Discipline	High TI – High PI	High TI – Low PI	Low TI – High PI	Low TI – Low PI
Community psychiatric nurses	40.4	15.7	22.3	21.7
Nurses (other than CPNs)	45.2	12.9	16.1	25.8
Social workers	6.1	33.3	15.2	45.5
Occupational therapists	24.3	32.4	13.5	29.7
Consultant psychiatrists	36.8	42.1	15.8	5.3
Clinical psychologists	21.2	15.2	45.5	18.2
Administrative staff (including receptionists)	48.3	17.2	6.9	27.6
WHOLE SAMPLE	31.6	20.8	20.6	27.0

Appendix 2

The Survey of Team Members

This survey was undertaken to follow up the earlier survey on the organisation and operation of CMHTs, carried out by The Sainsbury Centre for Mental Health. 60 teams were randomly sampled from the 302 teams covered by the earlier survey. Individuals from 57 teams returned forms.

The mean size of the teams sampled was 15.7 (11.7 full-time equivalents). This and other key features of the teams corresponded very closely to those of the full set of teams in the earlier survey, suggesting that the random sampling had been successful.

In all, 870 questionnaires were despatched and 445 (51.1%) were entered for analysis. The sample comprised 166 CPNs, 31 other nurses, 69 social workers, 41 administrative staff, 39 occupational therapists, 34 clinical psychologists, 19 consultant psychiatrists, 11 other doctors, 11 generic/support workers, 7 specialist therapists, 5 voluntary staff and 12 reported as 'other'. The latter included three employment workers, two care managers, a counsellor, a student nurse, a support worker and a worker on information technology.

The mean age of the sample was 39.5 years (SD=8.7). They had spent a mean of 11.6 years (SD=8.1) working in mental health and 2.9 years (SD=2.5) with the team. 62.5% of the sample were women.

Dependent measures

All scales were piloted, subject to factor analysis to confirm their factor structure, and checked for satisfactory inter-item reliability using Cronbach's alpha coefficient. The factor analysis led to the dropping of one item from the Maslach Burnout Inventory personal accomplishment scale and two sub-scales from the Occupational Stress Indicator (both of which had alpha coefficients below 0.7). The remaining alpha coefficients were:

Emotional exhaustion	0.89
Personal accomplishment	0.77
Depersonalisation	0.73
Job satisfaction overall	0.92
Achievement, value and growth	0.80
Organisational design	0.81
Job relations	0.73

Rees and Cooper (1992) found that the measure of sick leave used in the present study correlated highly with actual sickness absence ($r=0.96$).

Independent measures

Personal role clarity and team role clarity were measured using scales based on the role ambiguity scale (Rizzo, House, and Lirtzman, 1970). Internal reliability was 0.79 for the personal role clarity scale and 0.85 for the team role clarity scale. The two clarity scales were modestly correlated ($r=0.58$).

The personal and team identification scales were based upon a scale developed by Brown *et al.* (1986) with established reliability and validity. The order of presentation of the two eight-item scales was counterbalanced across the whole sample. Internal reliability of the team identification scale was 0.85 and the professional identification scale 0.83.

Analysis

Pearson Product Moment correlation coefficients were used to examine associations between interval level variables. One-way analysis of variance was used to examine differences across groups except where non-homogeneity of variance suggested the use of the Kruskal-Wallis test ($K-Wx^2$). Multiple comparisons were tested using the B-Tukey procedure or the Mann-Whitney U test.

Analysis of the qualitative data was achieved by two researchers working together to systematically create categories generated from the data. The case number of research participants was then used to count the number of references within each category. Both researchers (SO and TP) have experience as practitioners within CMHTs. Resources were not available for a reliability check of the creation of categories or allocation of responses.